D1710121

Special thanks and acknowledgments

Dedicated with love to my grandmother Virginia and my mother Diane;

to my family and friends growing up in Tucson; to my first teacher, coach and dear friend Gary;

to all my coaches who have taught me so much about living with integrity and humility
Coach Scurran, Coach Becky Bell and Coach Wright;

to my mindfulness teachers who have helped shift my perspective,
Valeta and Rolf along with so many others who have inspired me greatly.

To my dear friends Marcie and Karina who always have my back with their love and grace
and to Stephanie and Talie who have been so generous with their time
and creativity helping me finish this project;

but most of all...
my thanks, love and heart to my husband and daughters
who have changed everything for me ...

all my love, bb

How Do You See the World? by Banni Bunting
First Edition

ISBN: 978-1-7341347-0-4

For an accompanying mindfulness curriculum, please visit:
www.BanniBuntingMindfulness.com

HOW DO YOU SEE THE WORLD?

A BOOK OF MINDFUL CHOICES

By Banni Bunting
with illustrations by Teafly Peterson

FEELINGS

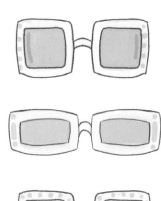

How do you see the world?

Sometimes,
I ask myself
this question because
I am curious,
and asking questions
helps me
understand better.

So, when you look around, how does the world look to you?

Sometimes, when I look around, it's like I am seeing the world through different colored glasses...

When I feel sad,
the world looks dark like
I am wearing glasses with dull gray lenses.

Nothing seems right.

I don't like this feeling
inside of me.

It is like time is standing still.

I am stuck, feeling lonely and lost.

Even the
funniest joke
can't make
me laugh.

Other times,
I feel happy as if I am
wearing glasses with shiny
yellow lenses.

Everything is sunny and
bright.

The view is beautiful, and I feel hopeful.

Smiling is easy
and feels good on my face.

Nothing
can bring me
down!

But oh my glasses can change quickly,
and I don't even know why!

Something that didn't bother me yesterday,
suddenly makes me frustrated.

I see the world through bright red lenses. I am mad!

Everything moves so quickly,
speeding by,
and I can't slow down.

When I see red, it is impossible
to keep my cool.

I say the wrong things.

I do the wrong things.

Then I get in trouble.

I feel out of control.

Then, my glasses change yet again!

Now I feel confident
as if I am
looking through
vibrant orange lenses.

I feel strong,
knowing anything
is possible.

I feel alive!

But then other times,
I feel calm and content,
like I am looking
at the world
through crystal-clear
glasses.

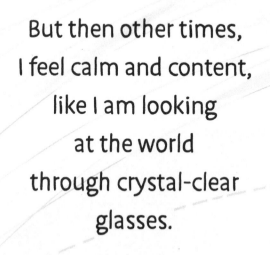

It is easy to see... it is easy to be.
Everything makes sense, and nothing seems to bother me.
I feel confident and comfortable in my own skin.

I see clearly.

GENEROSITY

COMPASSION

Being still and looking through
these crystal-clear glasses, I start to get it...

I begin to understand that there are many
ways of seeing the world,
not just through different colored lenses.

I realize there might be a different type of lens,
a lens that can help me with
all my many feelings, not so lost in color,
not so overwhelmed by emotions.

Maybe this different lens can help me with
whatever I am feeling, whether good or bad.

COURAGE

PATIENCE

RESPECT

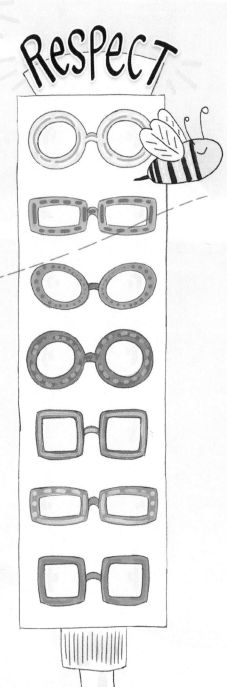

Maybe I could choose to see the world
through a lens of kindness.

Being kind to myself and others helps me feel happy even when I am sad,
reminding me that I belong.

Looking through a lens of kindness,
I feel closer to everyone, even people I don't know.

Kindness changes my view of the world
and reminds me of how we are meant to treat one another.

Or maybe, I could choose to see the world
through a lens of gratitude.

Gratitude helps me feel thankful for all of the good things in my life
rather than worrying about the bad.

Gratitude helps me appreciate the things I don't always stop to notice.

Looking through a lens of gratitude helps me see the world differently,
in a more appreciative way.

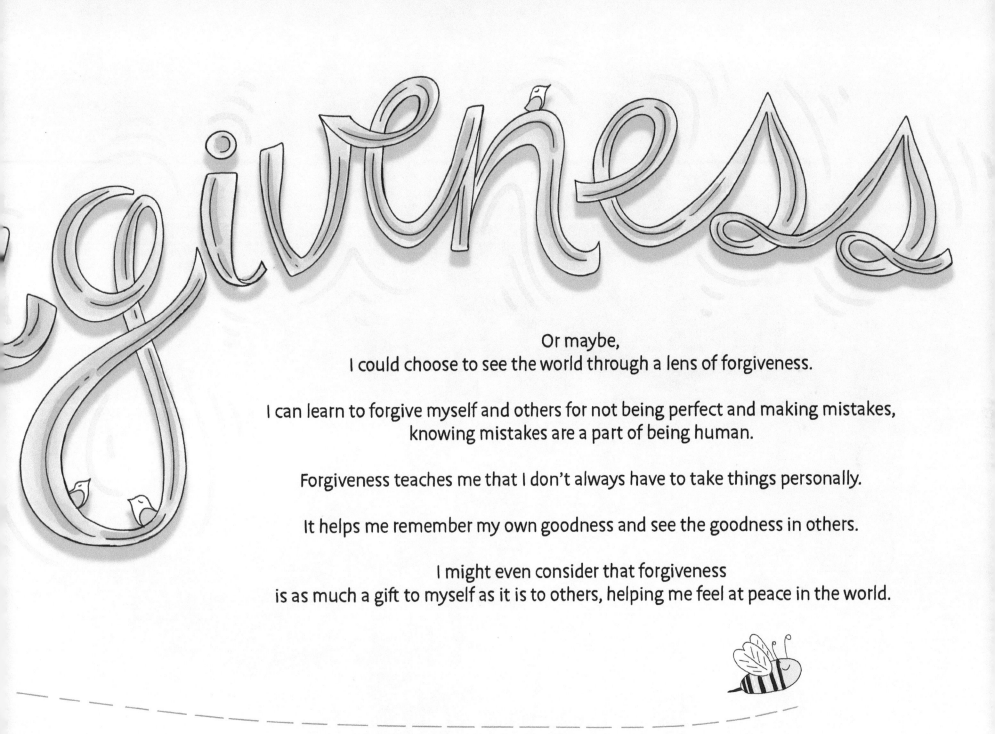

giveness

Or maybe,
I could choose to see the world through a lens of forgiveness.

I can learn to forgive myself and others for not being perfect and making mistakes,
knowing mistakes are a part of being human.

Forgiveness teaches me that I don't always have to take things personally.

It helps me remember my own goodness and see the goodness in others.

I might even consider that forgiveness
is as much a gift to myself as it is to others, helping me feel at peace in the world.

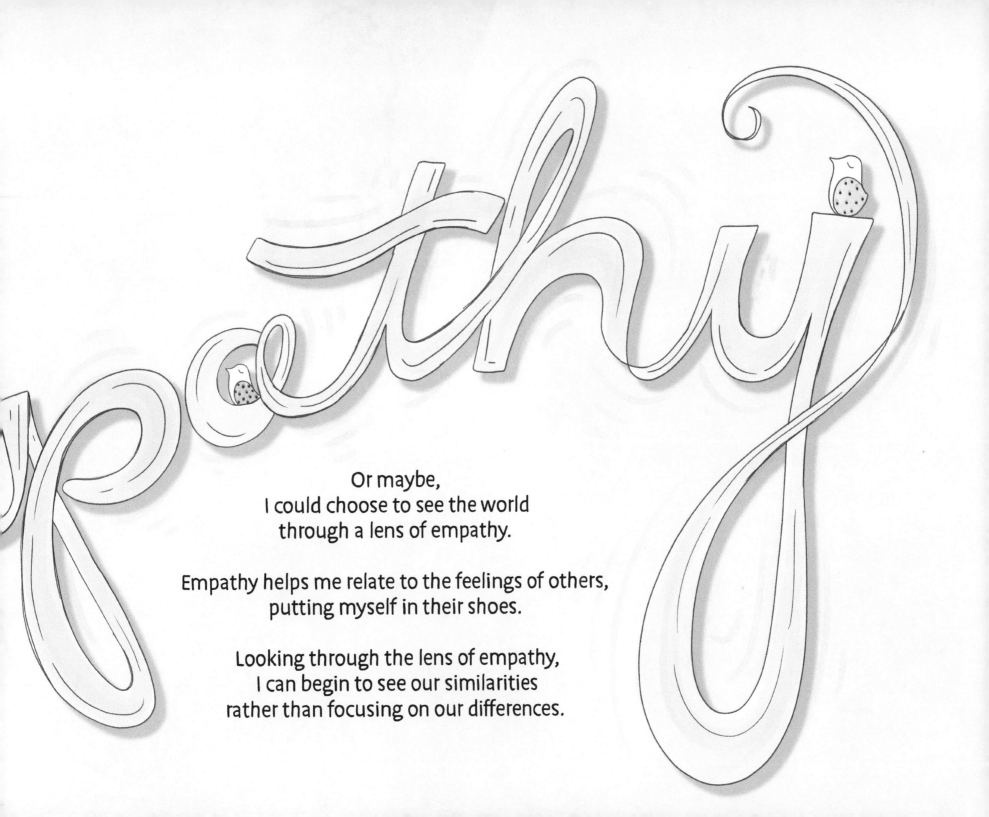

Or maybe,
I could choose to see the world
through a lens of empathy.

Empathy helps me relate to the feelings of others,
putting myself in their shoes.

Looking through the lens of empathy,
I can begin to see our similarities
rather than focusing on our differences.

WAIT A MINUTE

We're missing
one lens,
and it might be
the most important
one of all...

What
about...

Would we feel
more connected
to one another?

Would choosing a lens
of love bring
us closer
together?

So...

which lens
will you
choose?

How will you see our world?

QUESTIONS FOR CONNECTION

Use these questions to help deepen your conversation with your child and bring mindfulness into everyday life.

Kindness

Remember a time you said or did something kind. How did this make you feel? How do you think the other person felt as a result of your kindness? Is kindness something you can choose?

Gratitude

Can you think of three things you are grateful for and why? Which feels better... focusing on the good things in your life or focusing on the bad? Do you have a choice on what you focus on?

Forgiveness

Have you ever made a mistake? What was that like? Did you learn anything from it? Were you able to forgive yourself? Are you able to forgive others for making mistakes? Do you ever keep people out of your heart? How does this make you feel?

Empathy

Have you ever "stood in" someone else's shoes, understanding what they are feeling and going through? Is it easy to appreciate how others are feeling? What does it take from you to appreciate another's feelings? Do you have to pay attention? Does it help to be "present"?

Love

What matters most to you in your life? What do you love? What do you love about yourself? What do you love about others? What makes your heart sing? What are your greatest hopes and dreams?

HEARTFULNESS

Heartfulness, also known as Loving Kindness, is an activity you can do daily as a way of deepening your mindfulness practice. It can take anywhere from 30 seconds to 10 minutes, depending on how long you wish to spend.

You might try practicing heartfulness when you first wake up in the morning or as you go to bed, or maybe when you are feeling down. Heartfulness can help to lighten our hearts and change our lens in how we see our world. Sometimes it is fun to practice heartfulness while walking outside in nature, sending heartfulness to animals.

Give it a try

To practice, first close your eyes and gently place your hands over your heart.
Next, take a few deep, cleansing breaths and then begin by sending heartfulness to yourself.
Either silently from within or verbally repeating the following phrases, knowing you can repeat these phrases as many times as you wish...

May I be safe and healthy
May I be happy and kind
May I be compassionate and understanding
May I live with peace and ease

Once you finish, notice how sending heartfulness makes you feel. You can send heartfulness to others, including animals and pets.
May you be... or may all beings be...

Be creative with your words and phrases, sending out what you and others need most. And always remember to pause and notice how practicing heartfulness makes you feel from within.

May you too be peaceful and happy!

About the Author: Banni Bunting

Banni Bunting is a UCLA trained Mindfulness Facilitator as well as a member of the International Mindfulness Teachers Association (IMTA). Banni has trained with Jack Kornfield, Tara Brach, Diana Winston and Rolf Gates. For the past six years, her primary focus has been bringing mindfulness into the classroom working with local schools. A three-time national tennis champion, former FBI agent and now wife and mother, Banni currently resides in Bend, Oregon.

BanniBuntingMindfulness.com

About the Illustrator: Teafly Peterson

Teafly Peterson is a visual and performing artist who grew up on the east coast and adventured west. She landed in Bend, Oregon, which she has called home for almost 20 years. Teafly works in a variety of mediums including drawing and painting, filmmaking and photography, spoken word poetry and social practice. In the past, she created a stationary line for Madison Park Greetings, 8-foot tall puppets to help promote Earth stewardship for kids and travelling photo exhbitis advocating for equal rights for the LGBTQ+ community. Her favorite things include swimming, singing along to David Bowie, trees and rubbing her cat's belly.

Teafly.com

CPSIA information can be obtained
at www.ICGtesting.com
Printed in the USA
BVHW091946051119
562996BV00002B/2/P